The Bone Wars

D1515910

Praise for *The Bone Wars*

You put so much detail and expression in it, I felt like I was there, but glad that I wasn't!

Ethan Hansen age 8⅙

I loved it when they were playing tricks on each other.

Penelope Heitmann age 6½

I especially enjoyed the part where Cope puts the Elasmosurus skeleton together incorrectly.

Antonia Manzi age 5¼

The sketches made it more fun and it also helped me understand all the parts of the story. Some of them are really funny, like the 'chicken dinner' one.

Iris Deasy age 8¼

I loved the book, it was really interesting and I found out lots of things that I didn't know before!

Daniel Farrell age 7¾

What a Super-Saurus book! Loved reading it and what a page turner.   Anna Douglass (teacher)

My favourite part of the book is the scores, where you find out who found the most bones.

Jack Hobcraft age 6

I really like the pictures because I could see how things looked in the olden days and I like to draw.

Daniel Farrell age 7¾

An intriguing adventure, that expanded my dinosaur knowledge, one that will inspire, educate and inform all who read it!   Anna Cooper (teacher)

Also available

'What's so Special about....?'
Ankylosaurus
Coelophysis
Diplodocus
Leaellynasaura
Megalosaurus
Stegosaurus
Triceratops
And, of course *T. rex* !

Check out what's coming next
at the end of this book!

The

Bone Wars

NICKY DEE

Advised by multiple award-winning

palaeontologist Dean R. Lomax

First published in 2017 by
The Dragonfly Group
London, SW18 3HJ
info@specialdinosaurs.com
www.specialdinosaurs.com

1 3 5 7 9 8 6 4 2

A CIP catalogue record for this book is available from the British Library.

ISBN 978-0-9935-2938-2

Illustrations by Ian Durneen
Cover design by Jim Smith Design Ltd

Typeset by Ellipsis, Glasgow
Printed and bound by Clays Ltd, St Ives Plc

For my Dad

Definition: Palaeontologist

(pay-lee-ON-tol-o-jist) aka Fossil Hunter. A scientist who studies all forms of life that existed many, many years ago.

Introduction

If you think that the battle to be the best palaeontologist in the world sounds boring . . . think again! This is the true story of how two men started out as friends, but soon became sworn enemies, all because they wanted to be the best.

Was it a fair fight or did they use sneaky tactics to achieve their goal? Did they behave like perfect gentlemen or did they spy, cheat and tell tales?

Let's find out!

Meet the dinosaur hunters!

OTHNIEL CHARLES MARSH

Born on 29th October 1831

EDWARD DRINKER COPE

Born on 28th July 1840

Prologue

Who Does that Bone Belong To?

People have been finding fossils for thousands of years, but until fairly recently, they had no idea who or what they belonged to.

The Ancient Greeks and Romans thought they belonged to cyclopses and griffins . . .

. . . the Chinese thought they belonged to dragons. . .

. . . and some people thought they belonged to Roman War Elephants!

More than 340 years ago, an Englishman called Reverend Robert Plot examined part of a massive thigh bone, or femur. He had a really long think about where it came from, but found nothing to compare it to, so he

decided that it must have been part of a giant human, like the ones talked about in the Bible.

It was a mystery!

In 1824, another Englishman, William Buckland, examined part of the skeleton and jaw bone of a huge creature and called it *Megalosaurus* – but at the time he didn't know that he had found a dinosaur.

Part of the *Megalosaurus* lower jaw, with teeth!

Name: *Megalosaurus*
Say: MEG-ah-loh-SAW-russ
Meaning: great Lizard

It was almost 20 years before the word dinosaur, meaning 'terrible lizard', was invented by an English Professor called Richard Owen.

He had a theory that these very, very large bones belonged to a new type of animal, a

group that might contain hundreds, even thousands, of new creatures.

And how right he was!

This helped to change the way people thought about life on Earth forever. They began to realise that humans weren't the

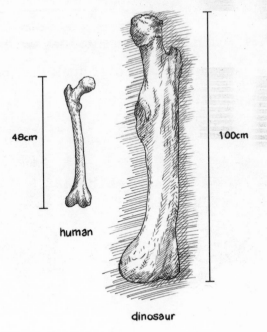

48cm

human

100cm

dinosaur

first creatures to have lived on Earth. Something had been here before, and looking at the size of a thigh bone fossil compared to a man's, something much bigger!

This is the beginning of a true story about two American scientists, and the very important part they played in the hunt for dinosaurs.

These two men met because they were both fascinated by all sorts of animals that lived a long, long, time ago.

Let's meet them!

1

The Early Years

Othniel Charles Marsh was born on 29th
October 1831 in a place called Lockport,

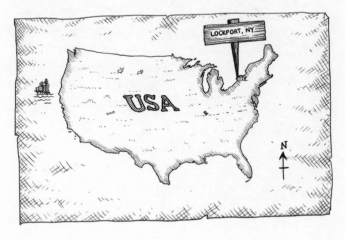

New York, which is on the East Coast of America.

His family didn't have much money to spare, so sending him to college would have been tricky. Thank goodness for his uncle, George

Peabody, who was a very wealthy man. Uncle George realised that Marsh was a very clever lad, and offered to help pay for him to study at university, and travel the world to follow his dream of becoming a scientist.

He happily paid for Marsh to go to Yale, which is one of the top universities in America, and then on to Berlin in Germany, to do a second university degree. Uncle George also gave $150,000 to Yale, which paid for a new museum – the Peabody Museum of Natural History!

In 1867, Marsh became one of the first curators, an important manager, at this Museum, so he had a lot to thank Uncle George for.

The other chap is Edward Drinker Cope, who was born into a very wealthy Quaker family of gentlemen farmers, on 28th July 1840 in Philadelphia – also in America. He was quite posh!

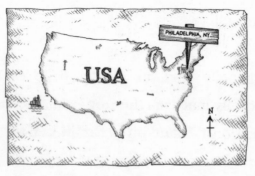

Cope was born and raised in a massive house with an enormous garden, so from a very young age he had plenty of space to explore, and he just loved to draw the creatures he found. He visited lots of museums and zoos with his parents as he was growing up, so he was never short of a new animal or insect to study and sketch.

The family had been farmers for many, many generations, but it soon became clear that Cope was more interested in animals and science than in ploughing fields.

He was quite naughty at school and would only concentrate on the things that he wanted to study, like science and animals. He also had a bit of a fiery temper and found it hard to fit in, so he didn't go on to senior school.

Instead, Cope stayed home from the age of 16, studying on his own and with his father, whilst reluctantly helping on the farm. When he turned 18, he began working at the Academy of Natural Sciences and his father paid for him to take classes with palaeontologist Joseph Leidy at the University of Philadelphia.

When he decided to leave home, his parents bought him a farm in the hope that, one day, he might follow the family tradition. But instead of working the land, he rented it out to provide an income for himself, so he could live in the city and work at the Academy.

Eventually his Dad had to give up all hope of his son ever becoming a farmer!

Cope loved writing, and the fact that he had left school early didn't slow him down. By the time he was 19, he had published his first paper, which means that he wrote an article about something new to science and it was printed so other scientists could read it.

This is a very important thing to do as a scientist. The number of papers that you

have published says a lot about your
knowledge and how well respected
you are in your area of expertise.

Cope started writing and publishing
papers at a young age and continued
to write throughout his life.

More about that later, as his papers form an important part of the story. . .

Let's find out how these two clever men met. . .

2

Meeting Up

By 1863, Marsh, now aged 32, had travelled across Europe, and was studying for his second degree at Berlin University, when he had a visit from a fellow American scientist.

Enter Cope, aged 23.

It wasn't easy to travel around the world in those days – you couldn't just hop on a plane

– so these two scientists were very pleased to meet each other. They had both grown up in America and had travelled a long way to get to Europe by wagon and boat. As they shared a passion for everything prehistoric, they got on very well. . . to begin with.

Did you know that the first car was invented in 1885?

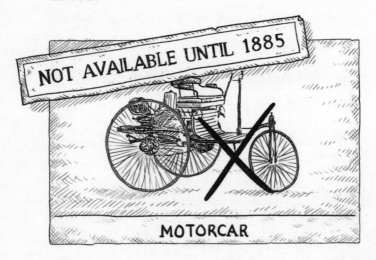

NOT AVAILABLE UNTIL 1885

MOTORCAR

And an aeroplane with passengers on board made its first flight in 1914?

NOT AVAILABLE UNTIL 1914

AEROPLANE

The most common way to travel when Cope and Marsh were growing up was by horse and wagon train.

AVAILABLE RIGHT NOW,
yours for only -$10-

(About 2 weeks' wages in the 1860s)

During the time they spent together in Berlin, Marsh showed Cope the sights of the city and they seemed to like and respect each other.

Great to meet a fellow American dinosaur fan, Ed!

Thanks for showing me around Othniel, I think we're going to get along just fine.

After Cope returned to America they kept in touch, sharing information and photographs

of fossils. They got along so well that in 1867, Cope named an amphibian fossil after Marsh. An amphibian is a creature that can live on land and in water.

In 1868, Marsh named a new extinct reptile after Cope, showing that they respected each other's work.

At that point they were friends, but all of that was about to change. . .

3

All Change!

The 1860s in America was a time of great change.

The American Civil War started in 1861 and lasted for four years. A very bloody battle between the Northern and Southern states about whether slaves should be freed or not. The farmers in the South wanted to keep their slaves to work on the land, but the people in the North

Confederate   Unionist

"Keep the slaves!"   "Free the slaves!"

SOUTH   NORTH

wanted to abolish slavery, getting rid of it altogether.

The North eventually won and the slaves were freed, but more people died during that war than in any other war in American history – over 620,000. That's a lot! More than the Americans lost in the First and Second World Wars combined.

After the Civil War, all sorts of things changed in America.

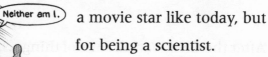

'm really, really famous!

Science was one of the areas that changed a lot, as the government gave huge amounts of money to hospitals, to provide proper training for doctors and nurses, and research into new treatments.

It wasn't just medical science that benefited, the new science of palaeontology became very well respected and talked about.

I'm not famous.

Many people wanted to be famous, not for being a footballer or

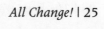

Neither am I.

a movie star like today, but for being a scientist.

Travelling around America at that time was tricky because of its size. America is 40 times bigger than the United Kingdom, 15 times bigger than France, three times bigger than India and about the same size as China.

1869 was a very important year in American history as it was the year that

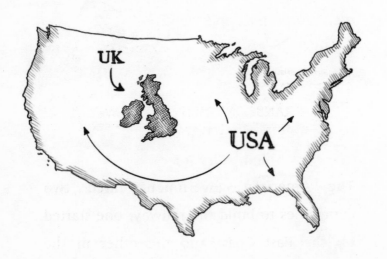

the transcontinental railway was finished. It joined the existing railways lines in the west to the new tracks, opening up the lands in the middle and the west to everyone.

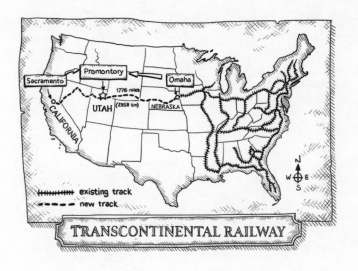

existing track
new track

TRANSCONTINENTAL RAILWAY

The American government hired two companies to build the railway; one started on the East Coast and the other in the

Midwest in Omaha, Nebraska. It took seven years, but eventually they met in the middle, in a place called Utah. On the day the railroad was officially opened, a golden spike was hammered into the ground, to mark the connection of the east to the west.

Journeys that had taken days now took only a few hours.

Much bigger and heavier cargo could be transported as the steam trains could take the strain.

That's me out of a job then!

The 'Wild West' of America was a very rocky place: hot, dry and dusty in the summer and wet, windy and chilly in the winter. Over time, the wind and the rain would wear away the soil and small rocks, revealing parts of fossils that could then be excavated.

Who are all these people and why are they on my land?

This area in the centre of America was to become known as the greatest fossil field on Earth, and the competition to find the most fossils was about to start. Even though the area was filled with danger from Native Americans who objected to the new settlers, as well as lots of poisonous snakes

and very harsh weather, nothing was going
to stop Marsh and Cope.

Sssssss...If they bring that lump of metal any closer to my family, I'll bite! I will!

And so the race begins. . .

4

The Big Falling Out

In the 1850s and 60s, most gentlemen scientists didn't leave the comfort of their museums to search for fossils, oh no!

Find me some fossils - and don't come back until you've found something A-MAY-ZING!

It's all right for him, sitting in his comfy armchair. It's dangerous out there!

Yes, sir!

These scientists paid others to go out and get their hands dirty, and send back everything they found.

Back in 1858, the discovery of a new dinosaur in New Jersey called *Hadrosaurus*, had sparked great excitement when it was announced, as it was the first really important dinosaur discovery in America.

Name : *Hadrosaurus*
Say : HAD-row-SAW-russ
Meaning : Bulky or large lizard

It was the first time that scientists had seen the fossil of a dinosaur that walked on two legs instead of four.

1868   Present Day

Palaeontologists now think that *Hadrosaurus* could walk on both two and four legs.

Megalosaurus had already been discovered in England, but scientists hadn't worked out that it walked on two legs yet. They still thought it walked on four!

It was studied by two famous palaeontologists, William Parker Foulke and Joseph

Leidy. They asked an English sculptor, Benjamin Waterhouse Hawkins, to come to America to mount the dinosaur for the museum in Philadelphia where Cope worked. This was the first time this had been done, anywhere in the world.

When a fossil is 'mounted', it is put together and displayed, so people can see what it might have looked like when it was alive.

Although this dinosaur wasn't discovered by Marsh or Cope, it's what Marsh did 10 years after the discovery that changed everything, and ruined Marsh and Cope's friendship.

When Marsh heard about the fossil he was very impressed, and asked Cope if he could see the quarry where this dinosaur had been discovered. Cope was very happy to take him, but this is when everything started to go wrong . . .

Marsh had a secret reason for his request. He didn't just want to look at the site, he also wanted to see what he could get from it. While at the quarry, Marsh bribed some of

the workers to send him all the new discoveries that they made, rather than sending them to Cope as they were supposed to. Naughty!

Marsh saw himself as a businessman and scientist, not a gentleman scientist, and didn't see anything wrong with the arrangement. Cope, however, was very, very angry when he found out why his supply of new fossils had dried up.

Then, Cope made a mistake that was so big, it is still talked about today. . .

5

Oooooops!

Cope was always in a rush to get papers published about his discoveries because he was worried that someone else might get there first.

When he was studying the fossil remains of a plesiosaur (PLEE-zee-UH-saw), which he named *Elasmosaurus*, he published his findings too quickly. A plesiosaur is a type of extinct marine reptile, one of the incredible creatures that ruled the oceans at the same time the dinosaurs ruled the land.

Name: *Elasmosaurus*

Say: EE-laz-mo-SAW-russ

Meaning: thin plated lizard

Elasmosaurus had an unusual skeleton which looked like it either had a very long neck and a short tail – or a very long tail and a short neck. Instead of taking time to check which

was right, Cope put the skeleton together incorrectly and ended up putting the head at the end of the tail. Oops!

Rumour has it, that as soon as he realised what Cope had done, Marsh contacted Joseph Leidy to check who was right – and when Leidy agreed that Cope had put the skull at the end of the tail by mistake, Marsh made sure that word got out.

Instead of admitting that he'd made a mistake, Cope tried to cover it up. He had already published a paper about this marine reptile, and although he tried to buy back all the copies of the article, it was too late. Everyone knew.

This was the big turning point in Marsh and Cope's relationship. If Cope had put his hands up and said, 'Sorry, my mistake,' everyone would have soon forgotten about it, but he was far too angry to admit he was wrong – and this made it much easier for Marsh to make him look bad.

Their friendship was definitely over. Their rivalry intensified and things were about to get nasty.

(Little did the two men know at that time, but Marsh was about to make a similar mistake, although this one was not discovered for more than 100 years!)

More about this later. . .

6

The Race is On!

The Wild West was a very dangerous place, so teams of workers, headed up by young palaeontologists, would go out to find the fossil fields, then report back to their bosses when they discovered something.

When Marsh heard about the vast bone beds in the West, where loads and loads of fossils could be found in one place, he decided that it was time to join the expedition.

He set off with a group of students from Yale University to stake his claim. He was not interested in sharing with anyone else, so he was desperate to get to the fossil fields first.

For protection, Marsh's team stayed close to the military forts which sat along the

railway, and used the railway towns for food and water.

This might sound like a great adventure, but it was full of all kinds of danger from prairie fires and storms – as well as the chance of dangerous encounters with Native Americans who were not happy about the takeover of their lands.

It was hot and dry and dusty in the summer, and freezing cold, snowy and icy in the winter. That didn't stop Marsh though! He wanted to stay one step ahead of Cope, so made his men work through the winter in very harsh conditions. He knew he was putting American science on the world map, and a bit of bad weather wasn't going to stop him.

They collected hundreds of specimens as quickly as they could and transported them back to various museums by train without taking time to work out what they'd found. It took years to sort out the bones so they could be studied properly, but Marsh knew the race was on, and didn't take time to label things carefully.

To this day, there are still many fossils covered in plaster field jackets – the wrapping used to transport them – sitting in American museums, waiting to be opened!

Cope felt very envious, as he was desperate to explore further afield, but the museum

in Philadelphia hadn't begun to send out expeditions at that point. This group of gentlemen scientists still largely relied on other people to send fossils to them.

In 1875, Cope's father died and he was really, really sad. Even though he hadn't wanted to follow the family tradition and become a farmer, he had stayed close to his parents, and had relied on his father's opinion greatly. His father left behind enough money for Cope to support himself on an expedition to the Wild West, so Cope decided it was time to catch up with Marsh.

Marsh had already claimed many of the fields close to the railway, so Cope had to find places to dig that were further away. He was warned not to stray too far from the railway as it was dangerous, but he insisted. He was told that he should take a gun to defend himself, but he refused. Cope was a type of Christian called a Quaker, who believed that people should live peacefully.

It was a risk, but he hired a team and set out anyway, as it was far more important to him to beat Marsh than to worry about an attack by Native Americans! As it turned out, Cope made friends with lots of the locals that he met.

In the meantime, in his desperation to publish more papers, Cope used the money from his father to buy the rights to the

scientific journal called *The American Naturalist*, in the hope that more of his articles would be published in it.

Cope became one of the most published authors in American scientific history and he thought that being so well published would set him on the fast track to becoming more famous than Marsh.

Did this tactic work? Not exactly.

Cope and Marsh didn't take the time to check what the other had discovered, which made a mess that took years to untangle. They ignored their former colleague and friend, Joseph Leidy, not wanting to hear what he thought of their antics.

Sometimes, they even wrote about the same dinosaur species – but gave them different names.

Think that's bad?
The terrible twosome were just getting started . . .

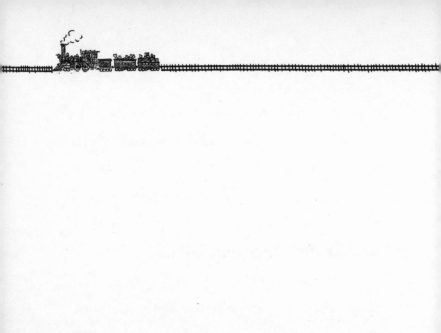

7

The Greatest Dinosaur Graveyard in the World

In 1877, both Cope and Marsh rushed to a place called Como Bluff in Wyoming, which was soon to become known as the greatest dinosaur graveyard in the world. At first, the area had been ignored because it was difficult to access and didn't look promising.

However, they soon realised that this area was a palaeontologist's dream come true!

The bones were just scattered across the ground, waiting to be discovered. Word got out that there were vertebrae, the bones that make up the spine, that measured nearly one metre across, and leg bones too big for a man to wrap his hands around! This caused great excitement.

Of course, Cope and Marsh couldn't work together, so they began at opposite ends of the 10-mile-long ridge, frantically excavating and transporting fossils back to their museums.

Wyoming

Como Bluff

10 Miles

1 Mile

These two men discovered some of the biggest Jurassic creatures ever found, revealing the lost world of 150 million years ago, when the prairies had been covered in lush forest.

There were plenty of new discoveries to share, but that was the last thing they wanted to do. This was not a good attitude, and one that would get them in a lot of trouble. Desperate to be the best and the quickest, they used every sneaky tactic in the book to stop each other's progress.

Both men accused each other of trespassing.

Marsh used his influence to make Cope's life difficult, even making it hard for his rival to find a place to sleep at night. Very nasty!

They hired each other's workers so they could find out inside information about their rival's discoveries. Marsh even had a codename for Cope – 'Jones' – which the spies used in telegrams to Marsh with updates on Cope's progress.

Marsh ordered that any pit he had finished
digging should be smashed up with sledge
hammers or
blown up with
dynamite –
just in case
any fossils
were left
behind!
We will never

know how many dinosaurs and other fossils were lost forever in the explosions.

Cope reportedly had a train full of Marsh's fossils redirected, and sent to Philadelphia!

They both put fake dates on papers, claiming that they had discovered a fossil earlier than

they had, so they could be the one to name it.

Marsh made his men scatter bone fragments from unrelated fossils around Cope's sites during the night, to make it harder for Cope to work out which bit belonged to which skeleton.

Cope hired 'dinosaur bandits' to steal fossils and information from Marsh.

Crazy times!

Then in 1882, Marsh used all the influence and connections that he had to make sure he was appointed as the Chief Palaeontologist to the United States Geological Society. With this top job, Marsh was in a position to make Cope's life more difficult.

Where would this battle end?

8

The Battle Becomes Public

At the beginning of 1890, the hatred
between the two men finally exploded –
and members of the public got to hear about
it.

What followed was a very angry war of words, as the two men fell over themselves to publish articles telling the world how rubbish they thought each other's work was!

On top of this, Marsh set a trap for Cope – but ended up getting trapped himself.

Marsh convinced the government to ask Cope to hand over all the fossils he'd found on expeditions paid for with government money. However, he hadn't reckoned with Cope's detailed record-keeping.

True, Cope had used some government money, but he had also used $80,000 of his own and could prove when and where each dollar had been spent.

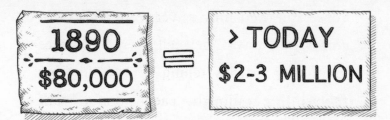

1890
$80,000

=

> TODAY
$2-3 MILLION

Not only did Cope have to return far fewer fossils than Marsh had hoped, the whole thing came back to bite Marsh on the bum! The Smithsonian Museum in Washington DC suddenly insisted that Marsh should return all the fossils that he'd discovered during expeditions using government money as well.

Unlike Cope, Marsh was rubbish at paperwork, so he couldn't work out which dinosaurs had come from which expeditions. He ended up handing back hundreds of fossils. He still had more hidden away at

home, but the damage to his reputation was done.

The battling scientists dinosaur scandal had become headline news in *The New York Times*, so everyone got to hear about the warring dinosaur hunters.

It had all gone wrong! Marsh and Cope were spending less time working on new discoveries and more time being nasty about each other. The American politicians who had given Marsh the very important position of Chief Palaeontologist decided that he was no longer the right man for the job and told him to leave.

Marsh and Cope must have known things were getting out of control, but they just couldn't stop themselves. Their war of words through the newspaper lasted for three weeks and by the end of it, both men's reputations were damaged beyond repair.

Was this the beginning of the end?

9

How it Ended

With their reputations in tatters, and their bank accounts nearly empty, both men were facing ruin.

Cope had to sell part of his vast collection of fossils just to be able to live, as he had sunk the little money he had left into a silver mine that turned out to be a very bad investment.

Marsh had to re-mortgage his house, as the very generous allowance given to him by Uncle George had been spent long ago.

Years of stealing each other's fossils, destroying excavation sites, and writing scandalous newspaper articles had finally led them to a very bad place.

Both men lost everything, including the respect of the scientific community.

Cope was the first to become seriously ill, but even though he was really poorly, he kept working until his dying day.

He was contacted by an artist called Charles Knight, who wanted Cope to help people see dinosaurs as living creatures by creating models out of clay. Knight would go on to become a very famous artist and sculptor in the years that followed.

They worked together for two weeks, even though Cope was ill, with Cope helping Knight to understand how dinosaurs walked and what they ate.

By creating models out of clay, Knight was putting 'flesh on their bones' – helping people to see more clearly what the

Clay model of *Stegosaurus*, 1899

dinosaur could have looked like when it was alive.

Right up to the bitter end, Cope was determined not to let his rivals see his work and asked Knight to hide his papers under his bed!

Cope died in 1897, just before his 57th birthday. He was well-liked and missed by his friends and family.

Marsh died in 1899 at 67 years old.

Until the day he died, Marsh was trying to work out which fossils he owned, and which belonged to the museum, but he simply ran out of time and died at home, on his own, in a mansion crammed full of papers and fossils.

He and Cope might have been two men who behaved badly, but they did make a huge difference to the world of science.

Let's look at the good things they left behind . . .

10

Their Legacy

Marsh and Cope's over-the-top attempts to become the best and most famous dinosaur hunter did have lots of positive results.

Cope is still one of the most published scientists in the world with over 1,400 papers to his name. However, he is remembered as being careless at times, often too quick to publish his work without checking and re-checking the facts.

Even after he died, Cope still found a way to challenge Marsh. In those days, people believed brain size and intelligence were linked – so Cope donated his brain to science, in the hope that Marsh would do the same, and their brains could be measured after they both died.

Marsh didn't accept the challenge. Perhaps he was afraid of losing?

Cope's brain is still thought to be preserved in a jar at the University of Pennsylvania.

Despite, or perhaps because of, their bitter feud, these two men changed the face of American science forever.

Even though their behaviour damaged the reputation of American palaeontology in the short term, the work they left behind helped to define a new field of study, influencing palaeontology into the 20th century and well beyond.

They left an incredible legacy.

11

Scores on the Doors!

So, who do you think discovered the most dinosaurs in the end?

Did Marsh's head start give him the advantage?

Let's find out. . .

Marsh's discoveries include *Diplodocus,*
Allosaurus, Stegosaurus, Triceratops,
Apatosaurus and *Brontosaurus.*

Triceratops

MARSH

- Name - *Diplodocus*
  Say - di-PLOD-oh-KUSS

- Name - *Allosaurus*
  Say - AL-oh-SAW-russ

- Name - *Stegosaurus*
  Say - STEG-oh-SAW-russ

- Name - *Triceratops*
  Say - try-SAIR-uh-TOPS

- Name - *Apatosaurus*
  Say - a-PAT-oh-SAW-russ

- Name - *Brontosaurus*
  Say - BRON-tuh-SAW-russ

Diplodocus

Cope's discoveries include *Camarasaurus,*
Coelophysis and *Amphicoelias*

Coelophysis

COPE

- Name - Camarasaurus
  Say - KAM-eh-rah-SAW-russ

- Name - Coelophysis
  Say - SEE-low-FY-sis

- Name - Amphicoelias
  Say - AM-fi-SEEL-ee-ass

Camarasaurus

Do you remember that Cope put the head of *Elasmosaurus* on the end of its tail? Marsh made a mistake with a skull too, but his wasn't discovered for 100 years.

Marsh's *Brontosaurus* was missing a skull, so he made one from plaster and added some real jaw bones.

However, this made-up skull was totally wrong and had to be replaced on all the copies of the *Brontosaurus* skeletons in museums around the world when the mistake was discovered in 1981.

Brontosaurus

But that wasn't the only problem that Marsh left behind.

Marsh's *Brontosaurus* was at the centre of another scandal, but this one was all about names. Here's what happened!

In 1877, Marsh described a nearly complete skeleton of a young, large sauropod – a four-legged, long-necked, herbivorous dinosaur. He called this new find *Apatosaurus*.

Two years later, in 1879, Marsh found the partial remains of another sauropod and

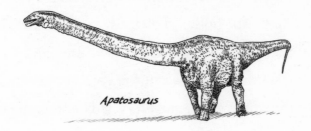

Apatosaurus

Name : *Apatosaurus*

Say : a-PAT-oh-SAW-russ

Meaning : deceptive lizard

named it *Brontosaurus* – a great name that referred to the thunderous, earth-shaking sounds it may have made as it walked.

In 1903, a palaeontologist called Elmer Rigg looked at both skeletons and decided that they were actually the same kind of dinosaur, and one was just a younger version of the other. As *Apatosaurus* had been named first, the name *Brontosaurus* wasn't needed anymore!

Then, in 2015, three scientists studied loads and loads of the remains of large, plant-eating, four-legged, long-necked sauropod dinosaurs and decided that *Apatosaurus* and *Brontosaurus* were different species after all, so *Brontosaurus* was back!

Name : *Brontosaurus*
Say : BRON -tuh -SAW-russ
Meaning : thunder lizard

Hurrah for the *Brontosaurus*! Marsh had been right, they were two separate species. (However, he did make the mistake with the head . . .)

12

The End

So, that just about wraps up the time in American history often called 'The Bone Wars' – and I'm sure you can see how and why it got the name!

Marsh and Cope did do a lot of good, and discovered lots of new dinosaurs, but imagine how much more successful they could have been if they had shared their work and talked about their discoveries.

At the beginning of the Bone Wars, just a handful of dinosaurs had been discovered in the world, but by the end, Cope and Marsh had named 144 dinosaurs between them! Today, palaeontologists only recognise a few of them, somewhere around 40-45. Still very impressive.

Greed drove these two clever men to behave as they did and when anyone talks about

Cope and Marsh today, they often remember the bad as well as the good.

Here is the wording on a sign outside Cope's old house, just in case anyone should forget!

EDWARD DRINKER COPE
(1840-1897)
Internationally renowned vertebrate paleontologist and zoologist, Cope lived and worked here in his later years. He wrote many scientific papers describing hundreds of fossil & living animals and is famous for his long-standing feud with O.C. Marsh of Yale.
PENNSYLVANIA HISTORICAL AND MUSEUM COMMISSION

Palaeontology is an adventure driven by mystery, and scientists will always want to learn more, so the search for prehistoric life still goes on today – although hopefully with more goodwill and fewer explosions!

Today, around 1,400 dinosaurs have been identified, but who knows how many more are waiting to be discovered – and who will discover them?

The End.

What's Next?

Have you ever wondered what happened to the dinosaurs 66 million years ago, why so many of them disappeared from Earth so suddenly, and if there are any dinosaurs alive today?

Well, wonder no more! Out in 2018, the next of the Special Books in the 'What's so Special about Dinosaurs?' series has all the answers.

'The Extinction Theories:
Where have all the
dinosaurs gone?'

Coming soon...

'What's so Special about...?'

Velociraptor
turkey-sized, feathered pack-hunter

Spinosaurus
large, semi-aquatic, fish-eater

Brachiosaurus
heavy, giraffe-like giant

Maiasaura
motherly, duck-billed herbivore

Join our Dinosaur Club
– it's FREE!

Each week you'll receive:

- Dino-tastic quizzes
- Games, brain-teasers
- Colouring sheets

Just visit
www.specialdinosaurs.com
to join and to:

- Enter the exciting world of a 3D artist and discover how a 3D dinosaur is created.

- Find out more about our experts and when they first became fascinated with dinosaurs.

- Discover what's coming next. . .

About the Author

Nicky Dee is a dedicated dinosaur expert and HUGE fan! Having fallen under the spell of these ever-popular prehistoric creatures, Nicky became so obsessed that she changed her career to write books about dinosaurs full-time!

Join us on Facebook and Twitter for the very latest news and details of Nicky Dee's tour of schools and festivals.

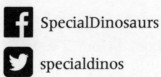 SpecialDinosaurs

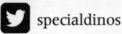 specialdinos

Get in touch if you would like Nicky Dee to visit your school

info@specialdinosaurs.com

Acknowledgements

Very Special Review Panel

I asked an expert panel of five to eight-year-old dinosaur fans, and some adults, to review the book before it went to print, as I thought that they should have the last word – good or bad! Fortunately, they had some lovely things to say and made some very helpful suggestions. Thank you for being so wonderful and encouraging.

Antonia Manzi   age 5¼

Daniel Farrell   age 7¾

Ethan Hansen   age 8⅙

Iris Deasy   age 8¼

Jack Hobcraft   age 6⅙

Penelope Heitman   age 6½

Anna Cooper   age 32½

Mum   age 60 + 12

Professional thanks to

Dean R. Lomax Talented, multiple award-winning palaeontologist, author and science communicator and consultant for the series. www.deanrlomax.co.uk

Ian Durneen An amazingly gifted artist who listened to my brief and interpreted it perfectly, helping the story to come alive in the minds of young readers.

Jim Smith A hugely talented designer, who worked on the cover design with Ian's illustrations.

Xanna Chown Professional editor, with a remarkable talent for remoulding and rewording, to make the best out of every sentence.

Heather O'Connell Mentor and expert at demystifying the print process. Couldn't do a book without her.

Debi Letham My very own Book Fairy, who coped with my last-minute tweaks and changes really well.

Chantal Cooke & Kenny Stevens PR and Social Media geniuses. Passionate about their craft, well connected and great to work with. www.panpathic.com

My family Wonderfully supportive, encouraging, patient, full of love and now almost as obsessed with dinosaurs as I am! Thank you. X

Also by Nicky Dee

Ankylosaurus
The Walking Tank. One of the most heavily
armoured dinosaurs of all time

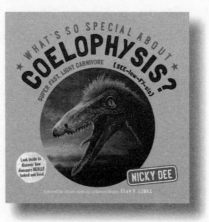

Coelophysis
Super-fast, light carnivore, one of the first discovered

Diplodocus
Long-necked, whip-tailed giant.
One of the longest dinosaurs ever to have lived!

Triceratops
Last and largest of the horned dinosaurs,
with one of the largest skulls of any land animal has ever lived!

T. rex
'The King of the Dinosaurs'
One of the most effective killing machines ever to walk on Earth

Stegosaurus
Plated, spiky herbivore with a brain the size of a walnut!

Leaellynasaura
Long-tailed, tiny polar herbivore from polar Australia. Chilly!

Megalosaurus
The first dinosaur to be named, anywhere in the world.
Discovered in England!

Don't forget to join the What's so Special Club . . . It's FREE!

www.specialdinosaurs.com/join-the-club/